"Patrick Dobson's *a successful disaster* takes readers on heartbreaking tour of the end of a long relationship. The speaker of the poems knows divorce is eminent and that like a "jagged knife across an apple," "time doesn't heal all wounds." The poems draw magnificently on the seasons and the natural world to heighten the reckoning the poet has with the loss of his perceived constants. Readers may recognize their own losses as Dobson notes "We huddle and wrap our arms around each other one last time before the end of winter and the beginning of new lives separate, incomplete, no longer whole." The collection is seamless, potent, and cathartic. It is a poignant meditation on the second half of life."

-Beth Gulley, author of *In the Margins*

"Self-examination is a type of excavation when buried in hardship. *a successful disaster* catalogues "Vagaries, challenges, issues, problems,/whatever they're called these days/piled up." Showing the extent one must go to exhume themself after the hardest Winter of their life. Patrick Dobson's poems unbury the heartbreak, disappointment, and reality of divorce. A collection of survivalist stories dug out of loss, estate sales, a parent's lament, and work injuries. An unflinching view into private disasters."

-Huascar Medina, author of *Protest as Love Poem*

"This book is raw confession, condemnation, requiem, and a lamentation of the dissolution of a marriage, the cardinal sin of divorce. This rumination is encompassing and unrelenting. In the yard a rose bush dies after a banner year, a thorny promise. Inside carpets grow bare, walls sag, the cold drafts in. A body succumbs slowly to the vagaries of age. A stout union dissolves in word play, "you do you, I do me," with no "we," creating "a chasm so dangerous to cross we don't dare." This is not a road map to resolution but a mandatory sojourn to all the other cardinal sins committed, omitted, demanding contrition. In the end resolution comes in acceptance of loss. "This could've been different, a life continued until death."

-Jose Faus, author of *Life and Times of Jose Calderon*

a successful disaster

Poems by Patrick Dobson

Spartan Press

Spartan Press

Kansas City, Missouri

Spartan
Press

Acknowledgments

Special thanks go to the editors of the following
publications where these poems first appeared:

"Falling" appeared in *I-70 Review*

The author wishes to thank the friends and family that
sustained him during the most difficult period of his
life. The list of these dear people is too long to list here.
But without them, the author would be a very different
and sadder person than he is today.

Table of Contents

"We're all spooks in the end."

–Pat O'Kelley

To Ken Larson, who taught me
all about the life of Job

Mortgage and Utilities

We stand on either side of the room,
a chasm so dangerous to cross
we don't dare.

Two positions, mined, fenced, barricaded
All the years' sleights and insults accumulated
infected with familiarity, our guild of two

By the time there's a new twist in all of this
incriminations and hatreds will subside
We'll collapse from our work. I'll stroke your hair

For now, I feel your heart beating
Love built the room in which we fight.
We will understand

Tonight, we'll sleep, but only lightly
Tomorrow, we'll begin, set rancor aside
conspire against the world, again

Sleep Deprivation

I lie awake, fear moments when
you sleep standing, frozen
fetching a glass of water
at the sink, your hand in mid air
like a catalogue model, stiff

You have fallen before
straight back on your head
dreaming as you were of mountains
streams, robber jays at picnic tables
of bringing your crippled mother home

I can't stand any longer
your absence from this bed—I know
your eyes are closed, your face relaxed
and run to you, a maiden in slumber

Tossing and turning, I dread the time
you fall when I can't be there
to catch you

Bullies

Sticks and stones can break bones
Words have broken my spirit

A run-in with a sidewalk, bike, tree
ERs, x-rays—splints, signatures on casts

Bones, three to six weeks—
I ached to escape plaster

Schoolmates never knew the cruelty
we exacted on each other

Names called, pranks pulled—
hoodwinked, tricked, hurt

A lifetime or forever or never
to heal a broken heart

Afternoon alone

Before anyone gets home—
appliances hum, clocks tick, dogs dream
yelps and half barks, rabbits under fences

An hour reading clears head fog
makes ready for television, dryer, slamming doors,
glasses and utensils in the sink

Clouds thicken, house grows darker
Tire whine, snowmelt drips on the ladder
three years on the deck
the last humps of white on the wood fence

As day winds down
fog settles outside
blankets neighbors in veils, ghostly—
tonight, freezing rain, sleet, then snow

We will walk out of the noise
into a sodden city—
all the living and dead wandering corners
shivering buckthorn skeletons

Loneliness Cuts at the Heart

A jagged knife across an apple
leaves skin torn and tattered,
interior serrated and raw.

You left two pieces shorn,
open and draining without a chance
to heal, become whole,
to pulse with the swell of desire.

Time doesn't heal all wounds
but allows the flesh to brown, desiccate,
form hardened, rough surfaces
over which to run my thoughts.

Looking out over the gray day,
I realize those years, decades, are gone,
melancholy, sad and contemplative,
takes over, flows where love

once coursed so full.

Deep Blue

The ocean's washed up against the patio door,
made me think of sea fans,
lobsters, scorpion and lionfish.

How deep those secrets
buried in trenches, between reefs,
spiky, cold, hard, hazard-filled.

Sperm whales and pilot fish and sea cucumbers
float liminal on the mind, creatures
find life hard in the open sea.

But we've come to swim here, in these waves,
in forests of kelp and constellations of sea stars,
to lose ourselves in anemones and clown fish.

Our journey takes us far from home.
We follow the water, head for the squall.
Our time is running out, the tide receding.

We'll live not to see the day the ocean
inundates our troubled souls
gives up its mysteries.

Divorce on the Plains

Plows are reopening highways
in western Kansas and eastern Colorado
after a foot of snow yesterday
stranded hundreds, killing one.

An unnamed company in county A
received a subpoena for information
it doesn't want to give away.
Now, the case goes before the Supreme Court.

Our lawsuit is stuck somewhere in that snow.
The prairie never gives up its secrets,
the citation for contempt lost to winds
rocketing off the Rockies.

Credit card payment, rent, threat of homelessness,
backpay only a promise and not something
we can retrieve from bluestem
drifted and buried below the poverty threshold.

It looks like clouds will be with us all day,
high of 24 and wind chill of 10.
The judge wets his finger,
holds it up.

We huddle and wrap our arms around each other
one last time before the end of winter
and the beginning of new lives
separate, incomplete, no longer whole.

Sunday

She worked overnight
twice this week,
slumbers late today.
The house quiet,
I hear her sleeping
and the boy in his room
hums to himself.
A moment before life
removes us from this paradise.

This Woman

Tending to the end of life ten hours a day,
she does paperwork more hours at night.
Up at 4 a.m., she commences again
punching computer keys and clicking links.

It matters little
that she receives no compensation,
dying patients always on her mind—
their pain, infections, bedsores, diapers.
They need. Their families need. The company needs.

She sits at the dining room table,
salad or sandwich and a cup of coffee,
long after I've gone to bed.
She's learned to get by with little rest,
her own health unimportant to her.

To what end? Her patients die,
leave trails of computer ciphers,
drug adjustments, doctors' orders.
She must be affected,
but then there's the next and the next.

This woman I love may just care for me
at the end of my life. Cancers,
halting neurological disorders, dementia—
she will be with me when it all comes due.
I can think of no better fate, no greater sadness.

Mild Weather

It's not been much of a winter—
a few freezing days, but nothing
to keep us out of the gray.

The rain has washed summer and fall
from the streets and into gutters
where the opossums rustle through leaves.

The natural world can't sleep,
has become a mess of restless insomniacs,
a populous tosses and turns,

nightdreaming of hibernation.
We imagine a cave where we hide
wanting things we cannot have.

We wander shirt-sleeve days,
cool nights, bare trees threatening bud,
wait for the snow to put us under.

The Coffee House

If someone asked baristas whom I come here with
they would say barrages of women, men with
    computers,
the occasional old man.

He converses for an hour or two, they'd say,
almost always sees someone he knows.
He's never with someone who looks like a wife.

He's a long-haired fellow who sits
outside when the weather cooperates
even marginally.

He orders cappuccinos, lattes, but, mostly,
he's a regular-cup kind of guy

Falling

Last night, you fell with a clatter
that started me from bed like a jackrabbit
chased across open desert.

I found you on the floor, confused, slim-lidded,
splayed, legs akimbo, lurching,
struggling with laundry fallen from the basket.

I stood over you, hands held out, waiting.
You flailed, determined to right yourself,
a ship listing in the ocean.

We were once so pliable, flexible, usable.
The house has grown threadbare,
carpet sprouting strings, buckling.

We have passed good years here, raised children,
experienced more successes than failures,
celebrated much with friends and neighbors.

Time has made old what was once new.
The furnace wheezes now, the cold flows
through doors and windows. We wear sweaters.

You were more embarrassed than angry
to have fallen again, to have lost balance.
I didn't know what to do,

couldn't act, impotent, unable to perform,
wanting more than anything
to make you young again.

Those Dreams

I pummeled and slogged
through those dreams last night.
I dodged and parried, feinted and jabbed.
My schizophrenic sister's lost her bike again,
I broke the gears, panicked fingers
couldn't piece them together.
I stood for an exam I hadn't prepared for,
didn't know about, hadn't remembered.
I couldn't find my pants for the interview.

Then, for the first time in 29 years,
I snuck out with a fifth of scotch,
drank until I fell down in the middle of Main Street.
Cops, spectators, old girlfriends, wife—a dream
    so vivid,
I sat on the edge of the bed
hand cupped over mouth and nose
to smell if it really happened.

Those dreams landed below the belt,
glances to the kidneys and lower back.
In the biggest slump since the market meltdown,
I apply for three times as many visas
than are available,
hoping one, just one, makes it through.
Sore, light-headed, I face a day unable to respond,
punch drunk, despairing of my efforts
to show my psyche it can't keep me down.

Roses for Virginia

The rose next to the front deck died this year.
Pruned too harshly, it gave up.
Stunted, thorny sticks plead with the sky.

I never wanted to plant this one, the dead one,
but she likes roses and wanted a few for the yard.
And a few I put in.

Last year was the rose's time. It climbed in its prime
to over six feet. Hundreds of small blooms
wafted fragrance over us evenings on the deck.

Its barbs pierced my gloves, drew blood.
Prunings on the truck, we dumped them
with the grapevines in the city mulch pile.

Winter has us in its grip, the ground frozen.
Come spring, I'll pull the dead rose
and send what's left to join the rest.

There will be another in the place
where the first arched over the rail.
It will grow and I will let it,
as I should all great loves.

Parents' Lament

Our son needs us almost not at all
as he roams from his room into my space,
his phone wired directly to his brain.
I tell him today we'll go shopping:
"Thanks, dad, you told me that yesterday"

An errand, a chore, but we'll do it together,
make choices of chips, pasta, fruit,
items to sustain a home.
Soon, he'll make these trips for us,
a man taking on the world.

Then, he'll be off to tackle life.
leave us with mementos, photos.
We'll wander our empty house
learning ourselves the hard way
what independence really means.

Work injury

Catching myself on my hands,
I heard the crunch
that brought the scream
Direct quote: "God fucking dammit,
I broke my fucking shoulder!"

The problems of being human
piled up and I cried—
divorce in the distance, another injury,
rounds of forms, forms for forms
What about my retirement?

Ms Bland delivered my mail
to the last two houses on the block
The police officer took the truck key
The ambulance hit every pothole
in this deteriorating city

Old men fall. Things break. They fail.
That is life, and I accept
my receding horizon
This work in progress
will soon terminate

EMTs unloaded their charge
rolled it to ER docs
Pain reminded me I was alive

Morphine, a silver cloud,
relieved me of gravity

For a moment or two
I floated above bed, monitors,
nurses, doctors, x-rays, scans
Out of body, out of caring
about job, failing marriage, fatherhood.

"Poor mailman," neighbors had said
"Your agony! Your suffering!!"
I didn't tell them dislocations,
broken bones, long recovery
were just additions to life's weight

Not an inch

Divorce—a cardinal sin, according to my father.
That and smoking, sending kids to public schools,
    drugs,
and not saying the Pledge of Allegiance every day.
Divorce equaled gun control, communist subversion,
tattoos, left-lane slow driving, and fornication.

I learned about sacramental wine
at Boy Scout meetings, cussing,
smoking, making my own decisions.
My life. I've done this to myself.
I left home long before I left home.

Mobs don't appeal to me, I quit the Pledge.
Two dime-size tattoos sit on a shoulder. I own no gun.
Denise taught me fornication's wonders. I drive slow
anywhere I want. I'm a Chin-forward Socialist Union
    Man.
My kids survived public schools.

I called lawyers today and didn't tell you.
Someone will deliver papers. My hands will be clean.
It's all business now, the complaints,
resentments, actions, and reactions irrelevant.
Divorce, too, is a lifetime commitment that doesn't last.

Cardinal sinning astonishes me, always has.
Transgressions are written all over my soul.
This is just another sin I must commit to find my way.
The world tilts on its axes, the tide rises. If I stay here,
I'll drown. I can't see the stars anymore.

The Ohio Plains

Shannon, the dental hygienist, comes from Ohio
halfway between Zanesville and the Lake.
I could tell. People raised on open ground
have a way of knowing the landscape

Our gaze settles on mice in the grass,
buzzards circling a hump of trees
where a homestead once stood,
Evening color blooms and shadows creep.

Above the dentist chair, past the parabolic light
a skylight reveals overcast sky. I notice at once
its gray enormity, the way looking
through a telescope reveals the vastness of space.

Her hands shove around lips, tongue, and cheek,
seeking out stain and small things
that turn to rot and pain.
She wields her pick like a craftsman.

Scraping and rinsing become background
for meditation on why we rise each morning
to clean teeth, carry mail, spend and save.
pay bills, keep house, feed kids.

Dr. Jessop comes in all bubble and glee,
checks Shannon's work, reviews x-rays,
congratulates me on good flossing.
Shannon smiles proudly.

I consider the sky above once more.
thinking halfway between Zanesville and the Lake,
to the plains hereabouts, to my tree copses
and mice and buzzards.

As I leave, she touches lightly my arm,
her eyes distant, focused on a small something
we both understand but keep to ourselves
The horizon lies at the edge of survival.

Nothing

It's nothing, nothing really
my mother said when pressure
of bills, kids, house dogged her
and her eyes, unfocused
gazed into a nothing I couldn't see

For decades my eyes focused
on countless worries stacking up
I knew the stability that comes
with having things to worry about—
at least I had things to worry about

Weight I could understand
an assemblage of pieces
If I can break the whole
into its constituent parts
each becomes solvable

Then kids, retirement accounts
workdays, laundry days, groceries
routines never deviating
a wish that someday
this all will end

On waking this morning
I looked in the mirror
saw in a far-away stare

my mom's eyes looking
into a future, opaque

into nothing, nothing really

Estate Sale

Rows of prescriptions, vitamins,
ibuprofen, acetaminophen, sleep aids
and melatonin—
old man tools for daily living

At doctors' directions, they accumulate
Accretions, land encroaching on the stream
When I was twenty
life had no heft, was light as down

The pills, potions, syrups, unguents,
salves and liniments
all have purposes
problems and pains
Proof of being alive

evidence of thousands of miles
walked, experienced, lived
They proclaim the truth:
There is not so much ahead
but much still to learn

People deny the process
of ever-accreting experience
and the end it brings them to
I dare not empty the medicine cabinet
take off on my own

My denial is full of shelves
When they are bare,
my kids will host the estate sale

Polar vortex

It snows hereabouts, you know,
as sure as seasons turn

But when it snows, we act surprised,
another once-in-a-lifetime phenomenon

Snowmageddon they've called it, again
like last year, the year before

A big, highway-side electric sign proclaims
"Where's your global warming now?"

Once, in a mountainside cabin
huddled at woodstove, I looked up

The thermometer read minus thirty-three
I shoved in another log, resigned to my fate

I made it out of there, down the mountain
to revel in whole fingers, toes, ears, nose

Dogs, I've heard, must learn
about snow every year anew

I'm not a dog, I remind myself
It's always been this cold before

Lame

Walk becomes hobble.
Whiteish, smooth connective
arthritis scoured away
turned my gait into limps and skips.

"Appliance" artfully installed,
will make this man walk again,
ambulatory, but never again a teen
shooting a bike into the sky.

Work takes its toll.
Cuff ligaments torn, one arm.
The other shoulder shattered.
Life is pain, they say.

Limbs contorted, I heft
a fork to my mouth like a shovel.
I will never again
reach behind my back

My children, embarrassed
at my shambling, my flopping arms.
Their father, jerking, lumbers
grunts, utters anachronisms.

An old man falls hands forward
to save nose and teeth.

He rises on the barely good knee,
finds himself insignificant.

More irrelevant every dawn.
He knows, despairs
He's out of touch, attempts
but finds no connection

He divides his estate
into meager bits
He calculates his worth
in mortal mathematics.

A low cloud

You're perceptive, aren't you,
seeing me deceiving myself,
denying denial?

The night in a campground covered
in a low cloud of cow stench,
you saw in me a man who could

step into a disaster, remain calm,
be the man you could depend on.
But without catastrophe, who was I?

We sailed the prairie sea together,
pledged our loves and lives to each other,
knew, somehow, we would make it.

That era passed a decade ago.
I was dependable
but without urgent exigencies

I stumbled into lazy complacency
and let slip things I most loved.
You are so far away.

We sign papers, sort finances.
taxes need to be done, and then,
we'll part, for now forever.

I didn't write this poem today

I didn't write this poem today,
not after two eggs and toast
with old-timers, our faces sagging
Not after meeting friends
failing in a failing age
Not after seeing you
talking division of assets,
custody of the dog.

I didn't write this poem today,
not after absorbing the fact
that marriage is transient,
seasonal as a dandelion.
Not after listening to myself
mumbling about starting
life again, for what?
The sixth or seventh time?

I didn't write this poem today,
not after facing disappointments,
sorrows, pains, grievances, sins.
Not after thinking I've collapsed
and had enough.
Why keep digging?

I didn't write this poem today,
not after swearing I've been
good at nothing but labor—
a thing of which to be proud
that nobody notices and is gone.
On my cenotaph, a name, dates.

No, I didn't write this poem today.
It wrote itself.

ancestral manse

memories haunt this quarter
ghosts, specters, people long gone
accidents and incidents
perfect walking weather
friendly people unaware
the dead dance in my head

at the corner of armour and broadway
a car piled up on a light pole
driven away to I don't remember
two days later, turning myself in
penalized—careless and imprudent
not felony dwi, good thing I hit and ran

central street between 36th and 37th
repeated bacchanals, tawdry sexcapades,
wakings in strangers' front yards
spent, puzzled, dazed
my only fistfight, ER stitches
that woman never loved me

more even, hundreds
remembered one by one
iterations and reiterations
ass-barings, chagrins,
self-promotions and demotions
shames and debasements

my walk takes me down
a dark street, faint recognition,
ancestral manse rises on the right—
nine decades my dad's family
sundays, weekends, holidays
we tore each other up there

a constitutional mends not all
oh, but for a new town!
a new slate on which to write
life without a past
where I walk empty headed
come home refreshed, unbeaten

levee

river bottom under cottonwood
melancholy shade draped
over sand even and fine as hourglass
here, as a boy, i daydreamed
sun flecks wandering on skin
dancing on river oats waving fists
at an oncoming thunderstorm

descending, lower, lower
painting sky emerald-blue
a shade half past dusk
the world shifted, i stood still
sounds of heartbeat, breath, leaf rustle
before the whole of creation
roared upstream

algae, fish, ozone aromas
anticipated raindrops big as nickels
burst of light noonday sun bright
thunderclap boomed in the chest
i ran off the bank, over the dike
to slip in the screen door, quiet
before uncle butch knew I'd gone

maturing, i navigated rhythms
life coursing through streets
up elevator shafts a child's vision

of friendly waters, benign creatures
paddle and navigated
rivers, streams, rivulets, puddles
finding, instead, rough patches, rapids

now and then, a river hawk screams
turns my head in memory
toward cottonwood shade
echoes under green-heavy canopy
sand soft underfoot, sound of waters
against a sandbar in a perfect world
the other side of the levee

John Birch's Dacha

Black-and-white Khrushchev
Pounds his shoe on the podium
tells UN reps that Filipino Sumulong
is "a jerk, a stooge, and a lackey"
Nikita dies of heart attack

Nixon apoplectic, red-faced
pounds on the Oval Office desk
denounces Indira Ghandi
"We really slobbered over the old witch"
RMN dies of a stroke

My dad, my general secretary, president,
retires at 54, drank another 30 years
pounded on tables, threw shoes,
lived on prejudices, denounced communists
died not recognizing himself in a mirror

His unauthorized narcissism
showed me what I'm capable of
"When you're a star, you can do anything."
I learned little useful from him
Except we're all spooks in the end

I prayed for your end
Letting god forgive you
What took you so long?
Did you goddamn walk here?
I just needed some names

Word of the day

Maturity, that complex array
of problem, logic, cogitation
best pursued in quiet solitude
I seem to know more about me
now that my time has slipped away

Self-awareness, an acrobatic feat
sensing the first strokes, twinges
onset of disease, anger, mental disease
understanding how to respond
instead of reacting—hard lessons

A child lost in the whirl of life
stumbled upon adulthood
reacted childishly, made bad
(very bad) decisions, blustered
mistook age for adulthood

Love, best known in experience
A grown woman at the bathroom door
naked, beckoning, desirous
of a display of affection
I've not missed the bus in 26 years

How much curriculum did I skip?
Sex and love, friendship, simple manners
the importance of shutting a goddamn door

The good china in the cabinet
gathers dust and retains its value

I should be ashamed, I should
and I am, who was that kid
who, blind, entered senescence?
I've come to know him and want to return
make him start fresh with clearer head

Lessons people, nature, life had to teach
I finally understand
My world slips away, I'm not ready
Fortunately, no one here
can sign a death certificate

Statistics

21,156 murders and non-negligent homicides
a number not complicated, but stats, you know
Guns, knives, garrots, smotherings, poisonings
cut brake lines, bathtub electrocutions
People get awfully creative when it comes to murder

They say there's a difference between crimes
of passion, anger, provocation, heartbreak
and cold, calculated, intentional homicide
But any man who commits any murder
must have exhausted all other options

He must determine his world
would be better without the victim
He's building a utopia, dreams of it
Get rid of this little problem
and I'll have the life I want

He tightens his grip on his lover's neck
Bewilderment in her eyes:
Is this really happening to me?
What transpired just now?
Must it all end like this?

I want half of every buck
that comes into the joint or else
She offers only thirty-two percent

and "else" happens, almost by itself
Another pathetic corpse

Murders, hot-blooded or deliberate,
all tawdry, needless, pitiful, sorry and sick
This woman's glowered at me all week, I'm afraid
She came home with plan prepared
Her utopia doesn't have me in it anymore

The privacy of the downstairs desk
might, I hope, mean the difference
between passion and a cold, calculated
knife in my side, icepick in my temple
My utopia depends on survival

Con Man

Senior-citizen days have arrived
My countenance, white face, gray hair
wise (?) smile, leathering hands
A man everyone knows loafs all day
A man everyone assumes is innocent

Loosed from youthful instability
my presence comfortable, smart
Young people give me credit
where none is due or just
They greet me smiling

They don't know what goes on
here behind horn-rimmed bifocals
how their acceptance and trust
gives me power I struggled for
all my youth and adulthood

They don't know, can't know
thoughts, imaginings, daydreams
memories of bodies writhing
steaming, panting on porches
park swings, in beds, cars, backyards.

The difference between citizen and felon
is the otherwise upstanding
never get caught for their crimes

Cops bought my excuses
let me stay on the street

An existence full of strivings
failures, mediocrities
My ambitions dulled, mediated
by what's still possible, what's not
Life is a series of dogs, they say

I soak up the acceptance for one
who was never considered
I'm an outsider, non-joiner, alienated
We can't talk, they don't want to, me either
I bask instead in their old-man ideal

The end of my marriage

Basement apartments long ago
were all right, nothing to speak of
Time made them darker
despite how many lights were on

With each basement life's horizon
receded ever farther
I worked, tried, sought

Thirty-five years I've not stood
on a chair to see out grubby windows
in foundation walls

She said I could move back
to an apartment in the basement
Our species, I said, should
never live underground

How Philip's lost leg saved my neck

I was losing my mind, what else?
Wife lost her career, sat bereft.
I applied, E-mailed, clicked links.
CEOs cocked their heads at my gray hair.

Diabetes got Philip's leg.
They gave him crutches.
My pain got lost between
his errands and appointments.

He made it up the front steps
a victory for him—and for me.
We celebrated with his cat,
rundowns of his favorite shows.

Ants on the brain gave me insomnia
sweats, worries about how the hell
I was going to keep goddamn lights on.
Remembering his tales put me to sleep.

Financial collapse takes no leg.
I got to keep all my limbs.
Phil's lost leg kept my head on straight
out of the end of a knotted rope.

Imagine!

Philip became an amputee, and I got to sleep.
I felt shame today when I told him
losing his leg five years ago
was the best thing to happen to me

at the time.

good night on a bad day

breeze sprightly, a bit chill
through the window
of this second-story room
aromas of spring, promise

just hours ago, a terrible start
how to get out of bed
the day's first conundrum
then, how to stay out of bed

forcing myself to shower
brush teeth, get out for a walk
and keep walking
goddamn boiler's on the fritz

cold shower, food, walk
a cup of tea—I have a stove!
a few pages of my book
delivered me to this chair

unhappy, but who isn't?
Jeremiah's home is the park
Ray sleeps in his car
this room, I have that at least

with the first breath of morning
I had a day, wretched as it was
it's a good night on a bad day
I'll smell spring again tomorrow

Life is a Series of Tents

The first one, the family model—
big, ancient, heavy, thick canvas
aromas of basement mold and smoke.
Family vacations, year after year,
dad pulled lines, barked commands
Parents on cots, kids on the ground.

Boy Scouts—smaller versions
of the family tent, just as confusing
with ropes, poles, floor canvases, flaps.
My first overnight at 11, I pulled out a skillet,
cooked potatoes and hamburgers on my fire.
Tall, strong Robert Rodriquez,
my tentmate, happy I was prepared.

Scout camp tents set on platforms—
wood staves laid on a frame,
poles permanently secured
when we showed up for ten days in the woods.
We had our own cots—ground no more!
Skunks and raccoons pushed noses
up between planks at night.

Backpacking tents, utilitarian,
waterproofed, lightweight,
carried with a man's life
in Missouri backwoods—

polyester replaced cotton canvas.
Trails through abandoned land
no good for anything but solitude.

The family tent opened
to mountains, crashing cataracts.
Boy scout tents to mature forest,
voices echoing under green-thick canopy.
Scout camp tents into the world
I defined, made my own,
luna moths floating in moonlight.

As an adult, I hike into isolation
only whippoorwills break,
into the Great Plains, down the Missouri.
Every tent, a step toward maturity
No tent is forgotten, can't be,
one leading to the other and on
to the one for the mourners.

Sirens

What I wouldn't give to have
Beauties draw me off course
with sublime lyrics, destroy me

It hasn't happened yet
The call has not come, I wait
patient with these vagaries

On rough seas, my boat leaks
The water's up over my ankles
I'm so goddamn tired of this

A million would solve things
People who say money can't
have more than they need

I'm here for them all open arms
and bank accounts
I beg, plead to pay tax on capital gains

Even if money causes problems
creates new worries, burdens, and cares
it'd solve the problem of being broke

For now, full- (even half-) breasted singers
aloft in the rocks and on shoals might promise
a gentle touch, something to die for

For the lack of carats

When we were married I refused
to indebt us for a diamond. A stone
bloody or not, common
sparkle in imaginations De Beers created

I found diamonds a commodity
like green plains of wheat, oats, soybeans
Common carbon useful cutting rebar
grinding steel flanges, abrading stone

No, an alloy ring, precious, then, by far
to a couple whose combined income
could've hardly afforded extravagance
beyond mortgage, utilities, taxes

A simple circle on our left hands
symbol of commitment, patience
durability and hope and dreams
patience and tolerance and love

Those have turned to disappointment
You say you see a man in hindsight
who aspired to be a nobody
a mote in the cosmos

Of lack of significance, I am guilty
The alloy band on my third finger

symbol of time now more precious
than all the carats on all the fingers

in all the world

The cherry trees of Fujiyoshida, Japan

I saw this place, Fujiyoshida at the base of Mount Fuji
in Yamanashi Prefecture in Japan, a country
that tried to destroy us in a black-and-white war.
(Wars are all monochrome, so far as I know.)
Fujiyoshida was in color, so this picture
must have been taken, in peacetime.

Fujiyoshida has cherry trees
like we have sycamores.
But we have no mountain here.
My Midwest a green place, mostly,
turns red/yellow/orange.
The color falls, leaves brown,
spiky skeletons behind.

As I've known it, the world's sepia.
How else would Fujiyoshida
impress a guy who, in contours
of his imagination, sees himself
a fat grade school kid
a coach shames into a sit-up?

Dreams flicker in color
or black and white, spanning old and new,
never mountains only duck-and-cover drills
a few naked nudes I once knew
nothing particularly interesting
except mushroom clouds.

it's going to get better

it's movie night tonight
a distraction, something
no horse track around here

I don't bet on anything
but my own reliability
I always do this sort of thing

long ago, months behind
rent, electricity, water
a woman mesmerized me

standing there dazed, drunk
nearly naked myself, lost
mysteries of the universe

boredom often kills people
heaps of dead line the path
to Everest's peak

to be bored you must be boring
I'm never guilty of that
alone is good most of the time

after this movie, I promise
I'll be more interesting
but I'm not dying on a mountain

Today is not a good day to die

I tossed knotted rope over rafter
ants on my brain, racing thoughts
unending anxiety, the state of life

That time wrapped in pain
The world had become pain
speculation, confusion

Emotional hangovers
make ropes on rafters attractive
I avoid excess

Tough times, hard work
Soon, I'll be through all this
Surely, myself again

Now, I'm overwhelmed
but have a choice
Today is not a good day to die

the lawyer won't take my calls

the lawyer won't take my calls
my schedule is tight, I've things to do
urgency is in the air, restlessness
how to file papers to end a marriage

we agree on one thing, we can't talk
going on three and some years now
a chasm dangerous to cross
we used to have much in common

but didn't—opposites attract, they say
poles held together, gravitational force
you did you, I did me, we did us
variables in the equation changing

uncertainties, we had no control group
did not know our baseline, never did
love clouded the field like a dense fog
we skinned knees on obstacles it hid

love insufficient to break brooding silence
passive aggressive attempts
to manipulate inconsistencies
to dance again in each other's arms

I should have known when "you do you,
I do me," with no "we" nulled the sum

your empathy lost, my weariness growing,
ne'er the twain shall meet, you said

that lawyer needs to get back to me
while we assent to division of assets
get it all on paper, signed, to the court
out of our hands, out of contention

a ship adrift

divorce has made my future opaque
broken my compass, stolen my sextant
every step leads to hundreds
thousands, millions of outcomes
that end foundering my ship

ancient mariners in their canoes
pirogues, ocean-going fellucas
knew enough astronomy at least
to follow stars, constellations
calculate distance in dead reckoning

what I wouldn't give for currents
an ability to read stars, figure my distance
know even one point in the zodiac
compute my position on the sphere
all my appraisements inadequate

direction, something to imagine
that's enough to start, put a foot down
follow that step with another
mistakes—changes in trajectory
it all leads somewhere

other than purgatory
where I wander in circles, aimless
there's no moss on the mast
I've lost the ship's log, can't know
where I started, where I've been

petrichor

though my second-story window
pours aroma of rain into the room
makes me sleepwalk, trudge insensate
toward my conclusion

promise in that smell, fertile fields
a drink, end of drought
a break in the heat, harbinger of spring
it will be a good season

as a child playing in a river bottom
rain womb warm, light as flower petals
echo of thunder, way off, dreamlike
cottonwood leaves shedding drops
I could run between

where did that warn rain disappear?
into adulthood, most likely
unable to be stashed in a pocket
an elixir close at hand to cure me

rain fragrance through a window
draws me inward toward wonder
drenches me in insignificance
reminds me I am one storm away
from my salvation

Seasons

For Deena Sweider

Americans say this
as if that sentence sat
waiting for problems to beset me
in the military school of life
and think, if I can survive this
I'll be stronger, better
understand why challenges
are there to begin with.
I know I'll be mightier, they said so.

But I've read Nietzsche in German,
know the old philospher meant
„adversity builds moral character."
Maybe that's true and it counts.
But I've been though plenty
have moral character enough,
all anyone could want.
I just wish the seasons of learning
were shorter and those of joy longer.

Never to have known

I shouldn't be here or near
I shouldn't even talk to you
I shouldn't've made that turn
on Broadway that led me
down to the corner of Armour
where I fell in love with you

It's in mourning I regret
having ever started with you
It's in mourning I see you
not as you are but were
It's in mourning I ache
to turn back the years

and drive father down
maybe to 31st and find
that woman I kissed there
a long time before I met you
a long time before the turmoil
a long time before we stumbled

When a friend dies and is buried
when the wound is so deep
when a dog gets hit in the street
when the grief is so grave
when you decide to end it
when I can't feel the sunlight

I want deep inside, in my heart
with all my soul and being
never to have known any of you
not ever

A disturbance

I was behind the wheel on the phone
You fight me, you won't get shit, you said

Here's how the conversation ended:
We'll talk through lawyers, I said

It's all right, the mayhem has ended
I'm freed from discussion

I pay for the privilege
It's sanitary this way

People assure me it will get messy
But I know what's out of my control

I'll be kind, loving, and tolerant
(Mental health, you know, is utmost)

I'll let the lawyers do the talking
make compromises you can't

I'll go to work, deliver the mail
place packages neatly on porches

There will be a little something
a dent in my equilibrium, a disturbance

wiggling around in the back of my head
keeping me up at night

These things are uncertain, after all
until the judge bangs the gavel

All sorts of oddities these days

Divorce on the horizon, surgeries
Days lost in legalese, narcotic hazes
Where faces, dreamlike
Fade in an out like uncertain phantoms
Memories instable as comets
Departing their orbits
To dart toward the sun
Sling into who knows where

Absurdities, indignities of aging
Still looking where I might get
Some cash out of all this
Nowhere and no reason to spend it
Life never slows, these issues
Pass into more, always more
It used to be a man's house was his own
Now it belongs to strangers
Ghouls range about with table forks

Such is the plight of a man
Increasing irrelevance
What was important grows
Distant, indistinct, my grasp slips
Henry Adams knew it, saw himself
Of another age, he had that at least
I'm not sure I ever belonged to an age
Not special enough, falling apart,
Forced to admit I've nowhere to sit

Gross neglect

The geology of the past reveals
Faults, rifts, plates flowing on mantle
There's no such thing as a driftless life
Always on the move, always changing
It slips from our imaginations
Based as they are on dreams

Tension releases in sudden bursts
Rocking the surface, wrecking
Everything that we build or try
Everybody's got a choice
Yet she still cares about me
Despite myself

Tectonics of relationships
Slow drifts from mid-chasm rifts
Plates clash, wrinkles arise unnoticed
Where is that man who could
Do the whole exterior
Maybe replace the gutters?

Water flows down divides
Rivers furrow crust, intrusions
Hardly noticeable until stepping up
From the bank, I see what I've lost
Accretion forms new land I'll never see
I was never able to prevent this

Erleichterung

Challenges, problems, issues
Layer up, drag
Overload the mechanism

A wife lost
Kids wandering
Deaths in the family

Age advances
Wrinkles at the eyes
Mornings, the needle on empty

Hope, broken expectations
Holding on is everything
Takes every bit of what's left

Then, all is lost or seems so
Bald tires, busted taillight
A thrown rod all at once

Under the pile
A thing at a time
Determination

A problem solved, another
The world brightens
Lightens, listens, shows love

Patience, a rewarding virtue
Life's weight begins to lift
Still, a long way from the end

You'll never walk on air
Maybe hover a few inches
Above the ground

Migrations

I didn't own my home even
when I paid off the mortgage
Kids, wife, dogs aplenty, fishes
childhoods, adolescences, adulthoods
time spent becoming
mature adults again and again

Fertile ground for us all
True human contact, release
Nurses help, tending patients
Writers write, helping imaginations
to become part of mechanism
Nurses, writers, relationships

I leave, close the door a last time
A house dawdles forever
in the back of the mind
influencing perspectives, decisions
We had our wedding here
A nest has emptied, we loved well

Open secrets no one can see, hear
but that linger in touch
of body on another, late nights
early mornings, cardinals singing
Garden grows untended, lascivious
home to all who must depart

Migrations, one hemisphere
to the other, seasons turning,
we fall from each other like leaves
There will be no death today
We mourn our losses
understand life in decay

Insomnia, a requiem

What is this conundrum? Baited
as it is with guilt, shame, remorse
nothing I've done to you, you to me
Vague notions, ill-defined angsts
Ants march on gray matter

A ceiling stain drills into cranium
bumps along rills as if this were
the finest ramble it could enjoy
at this time of night, clatter
Limbic comes to, zaps the gut

A new pill alleviates a symptom
or two or three, keeps me
on mainsail boom until it pushes
I find the deck hard, bloody fishy
filmed, scaled, flaked, and bleached

An old pill no longer prescribed
Withdrawal nervousness, bees
buzzing in anxious ears
I'm three inches above the mattress
A pilot absent flight control

Nights awake accumulate, ban niceties
Grandpa used to say, "Dau hast
Den Brooch an. Go inside until
you've found your new attitude"
But I never could find it

It all passes, sometime, I know
These nights stack up and I pass out
The police find me in Walmart
parking lot wandering, wondering
What all this was all about?

I can only hope insomnia
my lifelong oft-times resident
pesky, pernicious, corrosive
abandons me in the afterlife
and lets a exhausted spook rest

A prophet

This dickcissel, a prairie fence dweller,
denizen of tallgrass, forb seed eater
yellow-browed, moustached, white beneath
buzzes in flight, lands on the sill

Like Banquo's ghost, it prophesizes
a late frost, a time of challenge
for cherries, lilacs, apples, grapevines
people who hoped to warm hearts

all barren in the coming season
In lengthening days, we expected warmth
but have come too early, it says,
misjudged its migration

Absent love, we'll all pay in famine
Days churning—work, sleep, work
until punch drunk, we wake
drenched in rain, reeling

Virginia

You don't know how achingly beautiful
you are as you fritter life, escaping
contemplation, a look inside
afraid of ghosts lurking there

I am powerless over decline
We once raised kids here, loved
reveled in each other's light
We're missing the story of a lifetime

You wanted a farmhouse kitchen
I wound up distracted, running
My surveillance feed tells me
we faltered, miscalculated

We've fallen asleep on the beach
Sun burns our tender flesh
Our masks have melted
made recovery unlikely

Our bankrupt historical society
burned its files behind the jetty
We forgot who we were, left ourselves
only depths unknown, unknowable

Pain, a contemplation

Physical pain, the great motivator
Slows, speeds, halts, interrupts
Makes us understand
When all is lost, we still live

Pain, the great mediator, lover
Sharpens vision, alters, truncates
Presence in body and soul
What we want versus what might

Just last night, quadriceps sprained
ER doc said muscles torn
Nothing structural, soft tissue
Yet more sleepless nights

Seven months of pain goggles
Distort nights, days, self
Some live a lifetime of suffering
This will pass, eventually, maybe

To match pain with resolve
Our weighty responsibility
Keep desire alive beyond
Intolerance for discomfort

We stand to lose everything
You have seen those who fear pain
Young, middle-aged, old-cautious
Afraid to leap, dream, strive

Acceptance, the key, unlocks
Pain is us, who we are
With it we know we live, breathe
We deal with it, be it

Financial planning

My accounts, slim as a famine survivors
will carry me as far as I can walk uphill
on a midwestern jungle-hot July day
when the meadowlarks squealbuzz
off fencepost into bluestem

In the glass/pleather office, financial advisor
taps and taps and taps, scenario after scenario
whirling in air, time before my death
labyrinths of checked-box-numbers, forms
The man never tells me what I ought to do

My mind wonders in redbud branches outside
The fox in the alley, mangy-skinny, sharp eyes
A toad, a lunch, a snack on compost heap
Opossum rolls by side to side
What do Medicare premiums look like?

IRA, Social Security, Roths, 529, savings
thrown bones and Ouija boards
Unenlightened bureaucrats toss dice
There's Fate in the breeze, a ruffle
I close my eyes and drop a finger

on a spreadsheet line
That'll have to be good enough
for the fox, toad, opossum, that squatty redbud
A doddering boob, wringing hands, worrying
A perfectly good compost heap

Looking back/forward

Sixty-two years
meeting expectations
fifty in hard labor
This pressure cooker
is enough to kill this man
Almost has
Twice
Nooses

Time for something
that brings no accolades
rewards, recognition
Everything
for someone
anyone
else

Freedom
from goods and services
from money
from myself

Even earning wages
to keep lights on
has become
too much about
me

A lifetime

The thought never occurred
hasn't yet, this could've been
different, a life continued
until death

Hints, incidents, clues
adjustments, alterations
small a first, unnoticed
Now, nothing left to bend

Denials, oversights, turned heads
doctor shopping, pharma like groceries
full selection, pain killers perused
remedies for resentments, traumas

At the end, memories emerge
Twenty-six years, a happy eighteen
porch sitting, sparkling repartee
tent camping, frolicking kids

You call like an old friend
as if nothing happened
banter about bills, dog
wonder why I don't respond

You want your old lover
like he'd forget abuse
He's never forgotten
though he's forgiven

He's started again
fresh slate, new ground
a future less opaque
fuller, brighter, lovelier

You left me long before
I moved out, left you
I sit in a stranger's kitchen
trying not to remember

The Errand

Divorce offers two things:
       1. Divestment of car, house, bed
       2. Considerable energy for others

I'm done, finished, over
Expectations deflate to nil
No accolades, recognition, reward

I'll gather in bits my human needs
Time to give unfairly, no return
patience, tolerance, kindness, love

Annihilate envy, avarice, hate
No speck left gives me
a sack of understanding

What will become of me?
The path leads not always
to intended destinations

I'll fail, start again. Discipline:
ambition, determination, fortitude
practice and practice again

My errand to give completes
"Maybe never" is a long time
No time at all

Photographs, 2014

Here we are, the artist's studio
Evolution of creativity, friendships
All together over tea and cakes
Discussion lively, unending
Night is falling, pictures sepia
Losing color to twilight

Family trip, we are among friends
Cologne to Trier to Koblenz
In Luxemburg, the Winzer's cellar
Bottled art in the art of living
Of making livings, of work
Rain has come, an empty street

The train, twenty-three minutes late
Put us back a day, the pension
Dim quiet, clock ticks, a cuckoo
The Frau brings a platter, drinks
Dinner, bed, rising, rushing
Shining morning, gravestones

You and he, our son, and I go
Separate ways, we shan't be one
But for holidays, even then
Coffee, crumb cakes, banter
The art of deep, meaningful
Superficial relationships

Good days behind us
The rest bereft of warmth
Filling time, meeting obligations
Pouring over photos of those days
We share memories neath love lost
Wander among specters

A missile's arc

Fields barren now, soil's gone sour
No long supporting either of us
Sun shines on me, no longer on you
Air I breath forbidden to you
Vice versa ad infinitum

No diplomatic pill for prophylaxis
Cultural DNA broken, gone haywire
Acrimony beetles into New Tork
Tokyo, Frankfurt, Hong Kong
Our interests even to our demises

AI machines they call them
Configure trajectories to targets
Allegedly military, points to prove
We'll grind you into dust
We've seen this all before

An embarrassment of riches
Hospitals, schools, residences
Patients multiply, human rubble
Constitutional obligations foremost
Fireballs rise on every horizon

In Washington, Tehran, Tel Aviv
Dubai, Riyadh, Cairo, Amman
Egos are at stake, swords brandish
Negotiating tables, vacant seats
Glasses of water growing tepid

That year

The last year, the year before this
Clearer in the mind than any other
Fades, stacks up, life gets lost

In mundanities—painting house, gutters
Property taxes, endless morning showers
Forgotten teeth brushings, filling stations

Then falls, scrapes, surgeries
All the therapy to repair body and mind
Grown kids left, the marriage fell apart

Nasty court battles, a lone three-pointer
A judge bangs a gavel, proceedings end
We count our assets, consider new futures

Later, we look back over decades
Say to ourselves, foreheads scrunched
Oh, it was that year! Yeah, that one

Breakdown

There's a man on the pole
Praying mantis arms outstretched
Fiddling, cutting, splicing

Breakdowns in communication
Talking past one another
I have this, you have that

Defense Department on alert
listens to listing ships full of holes
Crews' panic sparked mutinies

The man in the bucket, thumbs up
A line is clear, a mechanical buzz
He joins his mate, an armada in wait

When you call, I think to myself
We haven't talked in a long time
I didn't hear what you just said

Augusts of years past

They say all the cells in our bodies
Change completely in seven years
Swapping out old for new and new again

I'm looking at these pictures of us
Nine years ago we were other people
And a half, just about, mere visages

I remember those sulfur springs in Yellowstone
The feel of the air after rain at Ronchamp
Twilight on the Missouri River that evening

We were all of us there, how different
We have become new and new again
A feeling, an emotion, a memory

Our continuities puzzle me, what's left
After the changes, an essence, we are never
Completely remade, washed out, flushed

These tatters, pieces, bits we hold on to
Spread among us like clouds where we exist
Long after our renewal has ceased and we dream

A successful disaster

A successful disaster this last year
Vagaries, challenges, issues, problems
whatever they're called these days
piled up. Now, if I try to climb that hill
I will fail, have failed, have despaired
We have come and gone, I'm a father
whose kids depend on him, not for food
not anymore, but for him himself—
A leader of sorts, a bastion of hope

I tell them if I sit down to write a book
I will fail. A sentence, however, a page
I can do that, build stories bits at a time
The path my father taught me becomes
ever harder to follow, I conquer nothing
I step back, take a deep breath, grasp
the one thing I can, participate
in processes, they are all processes

Events, incidences, moments build
into days into months into a year
where the stack of life's hay
too big for the truck, teeters, tips
I've not the not strength to make
bales that would right the load
I'm a one-handful-at-a-time man

Patrick Dobson is a poet, historian, and memoir
writer. He carries mail for the United States Postal
Service and teaches in the History Department at
Johnson County Community College. His previous
Spartan Press publications include *a brief infidelity
and other reveries* and *When the Titans Sleep and Other
Dreams.* He has published three travel memoirs. He
lives and writes in Kansas City, MO.

This project was made possible, in part, by generous support from the Osage Arts Community.

Osage Arts Community provides temporary time, space and support for the creation of new artistic works in a retreat format, serving creative people of all kinds — visual artists, composers, poets, fiction and nonfiction writers. Located on a 152-acre farm in an isolated rural mountainside setting in Central Missouri and bordered by ¾ of a mile of the Gasconade River, OAC provides residencies to those working alone, as well as welcoming collaborative teams, offering living space and workspace in a country environment to emerging and mid-career artists. For more information, visit us at www.osageac.org